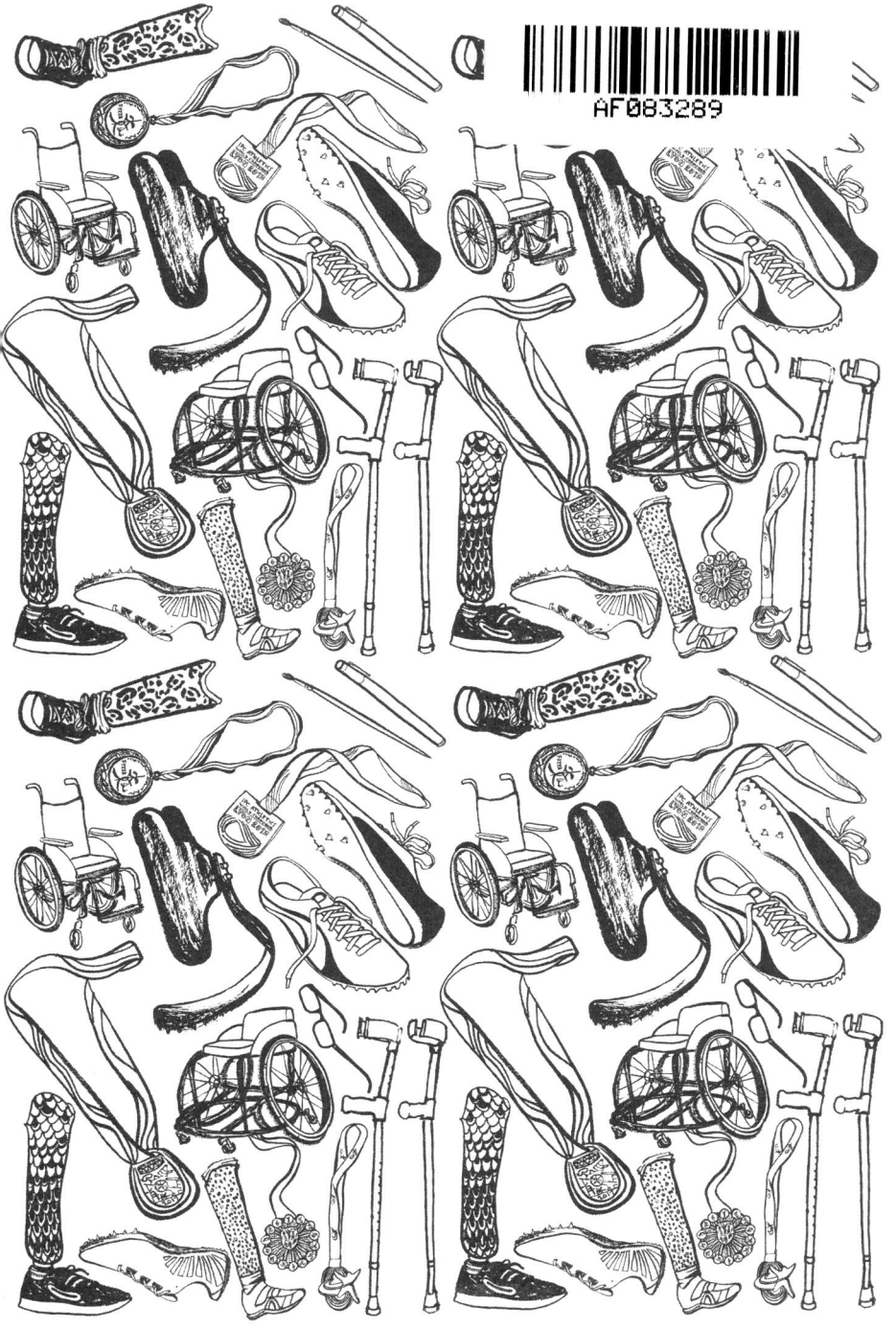

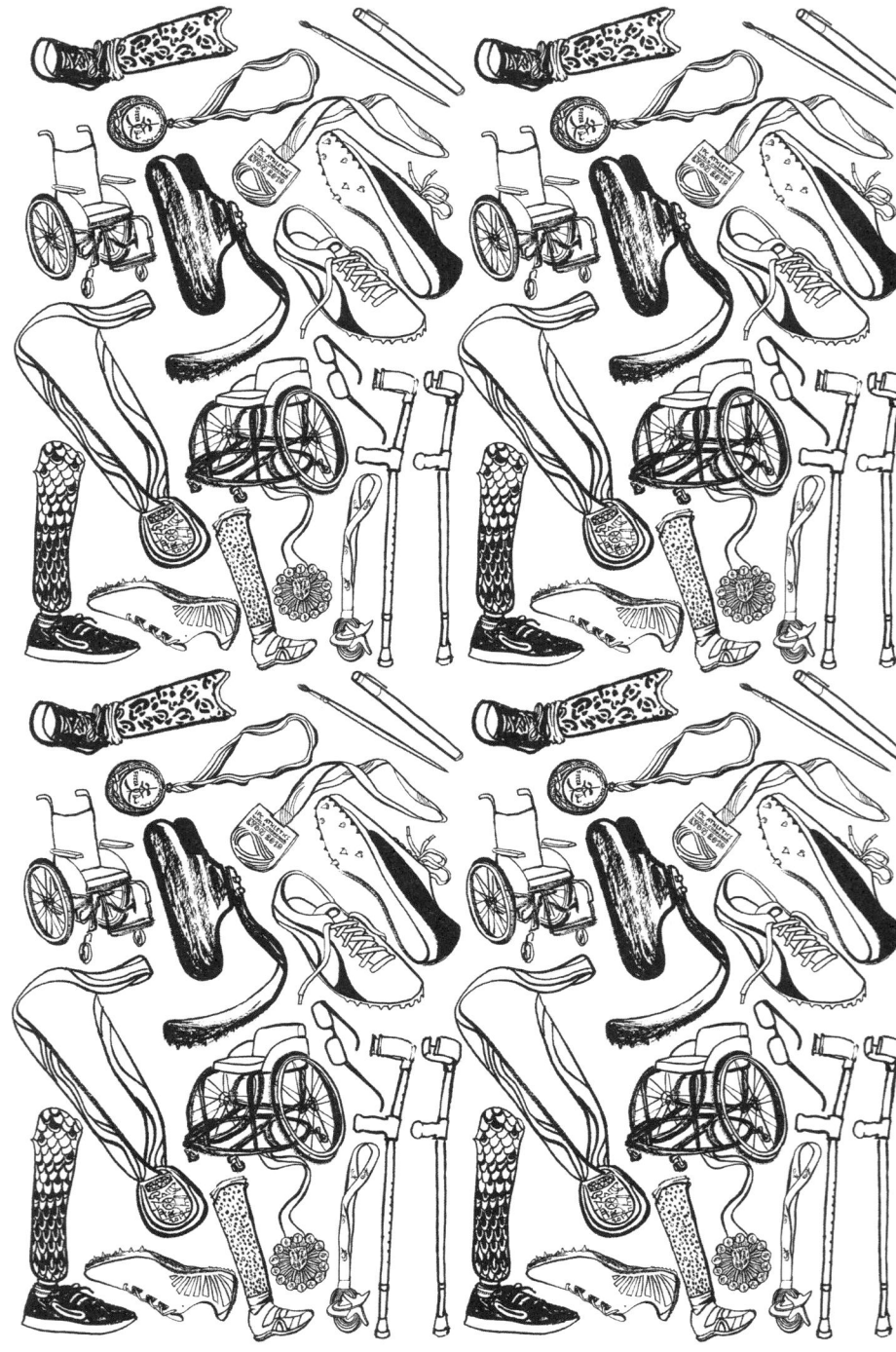

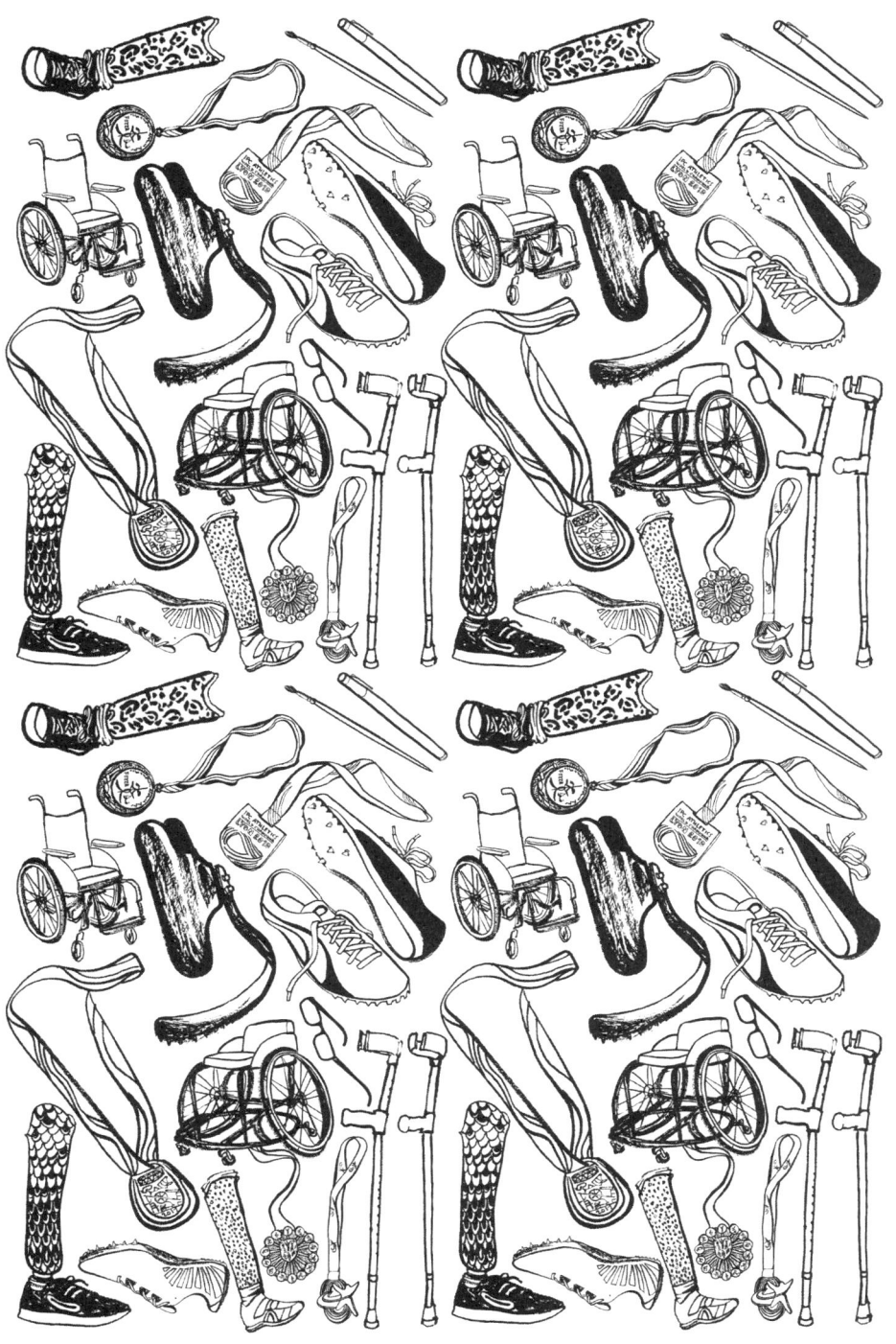

PLAYGROUND TO PODIUM

Sophie Kamlish

PLAYGROUND TO PODIUM

Collins

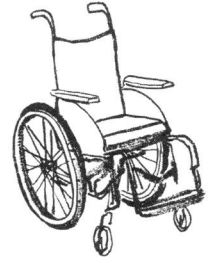

1. Celebration in Trafalgar Square!

It was 6th July 2005. I was eight and in Year Four at school. Our topic that term was 'London'. We learnt about the plague and the Great Fire and probably other things, but it was over 20 years ago so I've forgotten some of it. My class was on a school trip, and we were in Trafalgar Square. This wasn't just any old school trip. We were there, with thousands of other people, to find out which city would get to host the Olympics and Paralympics in 2012.

The choice was London or Paris. The news had been reporting that Paris was the favourite, so I was trying not to get my hopes up. I had no idea the outcome would have any major impact on me.

I was just a normal school kid who enjoyed climbing trees, watching TV and going to sleepovers at my friends' houses. I certainly wasn't an athlete. In fact, at that point, I was as far from an athlete as it was possible to be.

I had recently started finding walking really difficult. All my sporting exploits had paused thanks to my right foot deciding it didn't want to be a useful part of my body anymore.

Walking and weight bearing of any kind had become incredibly painful. This didn't come from nowhere. I was born with very unusual feet. The doctors hadn't seen anything like them before!

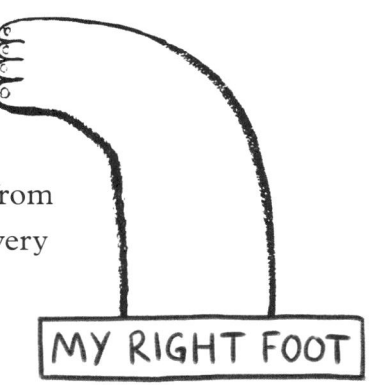

I had something called tibial hemimelia. The tibia (that's the big shin bone) on my right leg didn't grow properly, so my right leg ended up being shorter than my left. This meant that every time I got new shoes, my mum would send the right shoe off to the hospital to get a raise put on the bottom of it so that I wasn't walking too unevenly. Imagine a shoe, but with a special platform added, to lift my foot in the shoe. My right foot also curved inwards, so I wore a splint to try to straighten it.

I couldn't wiggle my toes and had no ankle movement whatsoever, which meant I had no calf muscle on my right leg. My left foot has an unusual combination of toes and is missing a metatarsal bone. These are the bones in your foot that lead to each toe: most people have five per foot, I have four. Despite that, it works pretty much the same as a conventional foot.

I don't remember when my right foot started hurting, but it felt kind of like my ankle was trying to burst out of my skin. Shortly after that school trip, I started hopping everywhere. My left foot did its best to take over the workload, but hopping around without crutches for ages just meant my left foot ended up hurting too. Then I couldn't walk at all! My right foot carried on being painful, so I got a wheelchair and green crutches from Great Ormond Street Hospital. This is where I'd been going for treatment since I was a baby.

MY LEFT FOOT

I had regular X-rays and my leg length difference was closely monitored so my shoe could be raised properly. I also went there to get my splints made.

Back to Trafalgar Square: I was having to sit down a lot, but I was doing my best to stand alongside my classmates to see properly. We'd all been provided with paper flags saying, "London 2012 Candidate City" and were waving them around enthusiastically in the build-up to the announcement.

Everyone went quiet, listening out for the result. We were standing beneath Nelson's Column and the watchful gaze of Britain's most famous arm amputee, Horatio Nelson. The second we heard the word "London", we, along with thousands of other people, erupted with thunderous cheers! It was the biggest and loudest crowd I'd ever been in, and it was so much fun being in such a massive group of joyful people.

It's funny to think that at this point, I didn't even really know the Paralympics existed. The announcement was about the *Olympic* bid, not the Olympic *and* Paralympic bid. The Paralympics were kind of ignored. If you'd asked all the people in Trafalgar Square that day to name a Paralympic athlete, most of them wouldn't have been able to – including me. If you'd asked me if I'd ever be a Paralympian, I'd have said: "No, I'm going to be an author and an illustrator. Also, I'm not disabled enough to be in the Paralympics."

No one had used the word "disabled" to describe me, the word still hadn't come up. I didn't identify with it at all. I didn't look up at Admiral Nelson on top of his column and think, *He's disabled like me.* My feet were *different* and that was it; I could do the same things as everyone else!

Except that wasn't the case anymore … *I* was the only one getting carried up the stairs to the classroom on my teacher's back, no one *else* was missing school for doctor's appointments or getting raises put on *their* shoes, none of my friends found walking super painful. But disabled? Me? Nah!

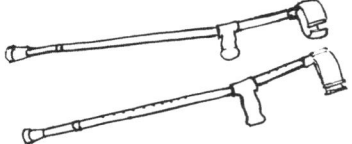

2. Let's go back in time

The Paralympics completely changed the course of my life. If you're wondering how this incredible, inclusive sporting event began, we'll have to go back in time to the Second World War.

Dr Ludwig Guttmann was a German-Jewish neurosurgeon – that's a doctor who treats conditions that affect your nervous system, including your brain, spinal cord and nerves. He's the person who pretty much started the Paralympic movement in the 1940s, but to understand *how*, we need to go back in time a little further. Dr Guttmann and his family came to Britain from Germany in 1939, six months before the war spread across Europe.

He was able to continue his work as a doctor and researcher specialising in spinal injuries at a hospital in Oxford. In 1943, the British Government asked Dr Guttmann to lead the National Spinal Injuries Centre at Stoke Mandeville Hospital in Buckinghamshire. It was the UK's first ever hospital unit for people with serious injuries like this, and treated many soldiers who had been injured in the war.

The spinal cord is a bundle of nerves that go from your brain all the way down your spine. The nerves sit safely inside your vertebrae (the scientific word for your backbone). Even though you don't feel it happening, every time you move, your brain sends a message down your spinal cord to tell your body what to do. If the spinal cord gets damaged, some of those messages can't get through properly. That means the brain can't "talk" to some parts of the body – so they stop moving. If there is a complete loss of feeling or control, this is called paralysis.

After a spinal cord injury, there's a lot of hard work ahead to improve or restore someone's movement. This is called rehabilitation (or "rehab" for short). Rehab is like training for a new kind of life. It helps people regain their confidence, stay healthy, and even play sports again. Rehab can include:

- doing exercises to build up strength in the muscles that *can* get signals – a physiotherapist would help with this;

- occupational therapy – this is learning how to do everyday things in a new way, for example: getting dressed, cooking, or going shopping;
- learning to use new equipment – this could be a cane, a walking frame, manual or electric wheelchairs, or using voice-controlled computers.

Dr Ludwig Guttmann set up the Stoke Mandeville Games to make his patients more active. He also realised that sport could help to improve mental health, not just physical health. The games started as an archery competition for 16 injured servicemen and women. It took place on 29th July 1948, the same day as the opening ceremony of the Olympic Games (which were being held in London that year). At the Stoke Mandeville Games, only British athletes competed, so it wasn't an international competition. But soon, other countries started getting involved and a wider range of sports were included. More on that later …

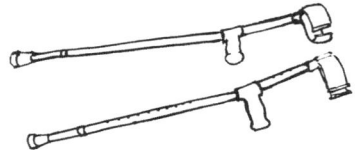

3. Finding my feet

A month after finding out London would host the 2012 Olympics and Paralympics, I was supposed to be getting my right leg lengthened. This can't be done in one quick surgery. It takes many months and can be a painful process.

In August 2005, there I was, in Great Ormond Street Hospital, about to get something called an Ilizarov frame put on my leg to make it longer. It's named after its inventor, a surgeon called Professor Gavriil Ilizarov. I'd have to spend ten days in hospital, and one of those days would be my ninth birthday. My mum, alongside normal birthday gifts, had also bought me ten extra hospital presents – one for each day, so there was something for me to look forward to.

If you're a bit squeamish, skip this paragraph! The procedure involves a doctor carefully breaking the bone that they want to lengthen. Next, thin wires and metal rods are attached to the bone. These wires and rods are connected to a frame which would surround my leg like a cage.

Then, every day, I (or probably one of my parents) would have to twiddle the mechanism on the frame which gradually pulls the bones apart from each other. The body is really clever and wants to heal, so new bone grows, filling in the gap. I wouldn't be able to wear proper trousers because of how big the frame was, and I'd also need to be very careful to keep everything clean to avoid infection.

The surgeon who'd be doing the operation was going round the ward checking in on all his patients. He got to me and found out about the trouble I'd been having walking.

He told me he could go ahead with the Ilizarov frame if I really wanted to try, but that because my foot was so painful, he didn't think it would actually work. Having a longer leg wouldn't make my foot stop hurting, and I might end up needing an amputation when I was older anyway. The alternative was to opt for an amputation. This wouldn't happen straight away, I'd have to wait six months, but the chance of complications was much lower than with the Ilizarov frame.

This seemed like the most obvious choice in the world to me. A surgeon was telling me that the long painful procedure might not even work … and there was a much easier option. I'd get to wear a prosthetic leg instead of a raised shoe and a splint … C'mon, obviously I was going to choose to get my foot chopped off! When people find out this is how I became an amputee, they always tell me how brave I was to make such a big decision at such a young age. I really don't think "brave" is the right word – to me it was just logical. I had a foot that didn't really work and was incredibly painful – why would I want to try to save it? I tell people it wasn't bravery, but they never seem to believe me.

The amputation happened on 9th February 2006 (when I was nine and a half). I only stayed in the hospital for four days – and I pretty much slept for the first two as the general anaesthetic wore off. When I first woke up, the overwhelming feeling was that the bandages were very tight.

I had access to a special glowing green button, and when I pressed it, morphine (a very strong painkiller) would go into my veins through a tube inserted in my hand. It was a bit strange – I could feel the coolness of the medicine going up my arm! The experience wasn't comfortable, but I wasn't in terrible pain at any point during my hospital stay.

When the doctors decided I was well enough to leave hospital, I got to go home to convalesce (this is a fancy word for "recover" after being unwell). I absolutely loved convalescing; there was no school and no homework! I watched TV, listened to audiobooks and drew to my heart's content. I did *try* to go back to school in Year Five, but it just made me feel too sick and tired, so I went home after lunch. I ended up not going back until Year Six started in September. I needed to sleep quite a lot during my recovery, and it was difficult to do that at school.

During my many months off school, I wasn't *just* napping and watching TV, I got my first ever prosthetic leg.

I think I had a bit of an advantage with learning to walk in it because I already knew what it was like to have no ankle movement. The fact was, walking was pretty easy. I didn't really see what all the fuss was about, and going to my physio appointments felt a bit pointless.

Running, on the other hand, *was* difficult. I didn't get it; my brain *knew* how to run, so why was my right leg suddenly so rubbish at it? My prosthetic foot felt like a heavy brick and was seriously difficult to coordinate. Eventually, I got the hang of it though. I was by no means the fastest runner in my class when I returned to school with my new leg, but I wasn't the slowest either.

My first leg was "skin coloured" and I hated it; it didn't match my skin tone at all! My parents took me to a fabric shop, and I picked out some patterned material for the prosthetic technicians to overlay onto the plain material that the prosthesis is made of. My second leg was red and gold! Even though skin-tone options are better now, I don't think I'll ever want a skin-tone leg, it's just not me!

4. The Paralympics takes off

Guess what? The 1948 Stoke Mandeville Games grew into what we now know as the Paralympics. Back then, it was held every year (not every four years like the Olympics) and stayed in the same place: Stoke Mandeville Hospital, England. But it didn't stay small for long.

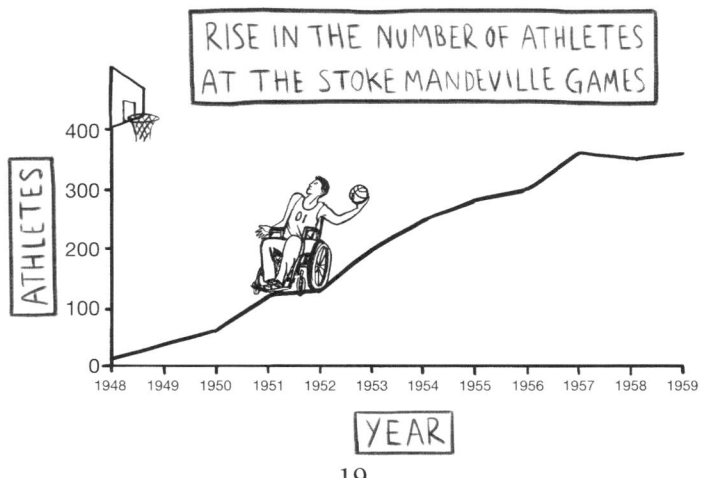

More athletes took part from hospitals across Great Britain, and eventually competitors from other countries started joining in as well. By 1957, 23 different countries were competing across nine sports: archery, shot put, javelin, swimming, table tennis, snooker, wheelchair fencing, wheelchair basketball, and dartchery. (Never heard of dartchery? It's a combination of darts and archery.) Not all these sports made it into today's event programme!

Everything changed in 1960. That year, the Games moved to Rome, Italy, the same host city as the Olympics Games, and 400 athletes from 23 countries took part. Dr Ludwig Guttmann's dream of an "Olympic Games for people with disabilities" was starting to come true.

At first, only wheelchair users were allowed to compete. But in the 1976 Games in Toronto, Canada, athletes with other types of disabilities were finally included. The number of participants expanded: 1,271 athletes from 41 countries took part that year.

Surprisingly, it wasn't until 1988 that the event was officially called the "Paralympics". Lots of people assume that "para" refers to *paraplegic* (someone who's unable to voluntarily move the lower part of their body), but it doesn't. It actually comes from the Greek word *para*, meaning "alongside". Just like *parallel lines* in maths, the Paralympics run alongside the Olympics.

So, from Rome 1960 onwards, the Paralympics were held in the same city as the Olympics, right? Unfortunately, this was not the case! The tradition continued in 1964 where both events were held in Tokyo, Japan, but it wasn't until 1988 that the Olympics and Paralympics were properly reunited again. There were many different reasons for this, generally to do with financial and logistical problems; there were often no accessible places for the athletes to stay.

Mexico City (the capital of Mexico) had planned to host both the 1968 Olympic and Paralympic Games. However, with just two years to go, they had to pull out of hosting the Paralympics due to "technical difficulties" (including not enough money and lack of accessibility).

In the end, the Games were hosted over 11,000 kilometres away in Tel Aviv, Israel, where around 750 athletes competed from 28 countries.

The 1988 Games, held in Seoul, South Korea, were a big turning point for the Paralympics. Around 3,042 athletes competed from 60 countries, and after 24 years of separation, the Olympics and Paralympics were finally reunited. And it stayed that way! However, it wasn't until 2001 that an official agreement was signed by the International Olympic Committee and the International Paralympic Committee, ensuring that the Paralympics would use the same venues as the Olympics.

It does seem a shame that it took so long for the "one bid, one city" agreement to be set in stone. Views towards disabled people have gradually become less negative over time, but there is still a long way to go.

For me, it felt like the Paralympic Games were treated like a bit of a nuisance for so many years, and accessibility for the athletes was not seen as an important factor when it came to the organisation process.

Even if they're not hosting the Games, countries need to invest in access at grassroots level (in local, community-based clubs), not just at the elite level. A study from 2024 found that in the UK, 75% of disabled children don't have regular access to PE. Schools and sports clubs need training and equipment to ensure every disabled child can participate fully in sport, not just sit on the sideline or be stuck in goal (unless they love being in goal, of course!). Not every disabled child wants to grow up to be a Paralympian, but sport can bring so much more than medals; it's about being part of a community, making friends, and maintaining good mental and physical health.

When disabled people aren't offered the same facilities as non-disabled people, or are treated as inferior to non-disabled people, this type of discrimination is called "ableism".

5. Fantastic gymnastics

I managed to avoid ableism for quite a few years as a child. Teachers at my primary school made sure I was able to participate in PE and when I went to gymnastics club, the instructors never talked down to me.

I used to love gymnastics – everything about it was brilliant. The trampoline was 100 times bouncier than any I'd been on in a friend's garden and the foam pit was ridiculously fun to land in. The floor was springy, which somehow made even walking more exciting. My upper body strength meant I could impress the instructors with how many chin-ups I could do.

There was one part I didn't love, though – the warm-up. The first ten minutes of every session were spent running non-stop. It was exhausting. My lungs felt like they might burst, and my legs would start to feel like lead. Then came the stretching, which I found incredibly dull. I was so flexible, I could never feel anything actually stretch. I noticed the other kids struggling to get their legs into certain positions and assumed I must be doing things wrong, so I copied everyone and winced like it was painful.

Later I found out I have something called hypermobility, which basically means my joints are a bit bendier than most people. Luckily, it's never caused me major problems, but for some people it can be painful and make injuries more likely.

I always knew I'd never be an elite-level gymnast. When the rules for competing are so strict that you can lose marks for not pointing your toes, it would be silly to even try to compete with non-disabled gymnasts. That didn't upset me, though. I happily attended a weekly class throughout primary school.

Having a prosthetic leg didn't massively impact the way I performed in gymnastics. If anything, my fake leg made things quite a lot easier. Previously I couldn't wear my raised shoe during the classes, so I was having to do everything with a leg length difference, which can cause back problems – now I didn't have to worry about that!

There was, however, one new issue: my leg flying off.

After recovering from surgery and getting a new leg, I was able to get back to one of my favourite hobbies: perfecting the art of the cartwheel. I'd practise in the living room, the school playground, the park, and of course, at gymnastics.

The problem was, when you get your first prosthetic, it doesn't fit for long. As the swelling in your stump goes down, the shape changes, so the socket loosens over time.

That meant that if I did multiple cartwheels in a row, my prosthetic leg would sometimes fly off.

I loved seeing how far I could make it go.

It happened in gymnastics once, and an instructor had to sit out of the lesson for a bit because they didn't know I was an amputee, and they thought it was my real leg, flying through the air!

Gymnastics is not a Paralympic sport yet, but I really think it should be. The events could be adapted – disabled athletes are brilliant at that. I'd love to see an amputee on the beam, someone with a visual impairment doing a pommel routine, or a wheelchair user on the rings.

The Olympics has 35 different sports, while the Paralympics has 23. The winter Olympics has 16 disciplines, and the winter Paralympics only has six (no ice skating or sliding events of any kind). It's a lengthy and complicated process to get a new sport accepted into the Paralympic programme; it relies on it already being an existing Olympic sport, as well as demonstrating a high level of participation across all five Olympic continents.

Let's see skateboarding, gymnastics, surfing and WCMX included for Paralympians. WCMX is like Freestyle BMX, where the athletes perform amazing tricks in a skate park – except they're not on a bike, they're in a wheelchair!

The Paralympics is still growing, so hopefully one day we will get to see disabled gymnasts shine.

6. Funding the future

The 1996 Olympics was held in Atlanta, US. The British Paralympic team came fourth in the medal table, winning a total of 122 medals – 39 of them were gold! The Olympic team didn't do so well. They were thirty-sixth in the medal table, and won one gold. At that time there wasn't any central funding for British athletes. However, the poor performance by British athletes in the Olympics meant this was about to change.

The very next year, the British Government introduced funding for sport. This meant that the money raised would be used to support all British athletes.

Before this, athletes often had to juggle full-time jobs alongside their training. With the new funding, they could train full time, afford better coaching, get more advanced equipment like wheelchairs or prosthetics, and access state-of-the-art facilities and prompt medical care. They could also afford to travel to different countries to compete. It made a huge difference, and soon British Olympians and Paralympians began winning more medals.

There is still a need to increase investment, or the Paralympics won't be able to grow and thrive. A city that is lucky enough to host the Paralympics becomes more accessible, and that means the disabled people who live there all-year-round benefit from the updated infrastructure, as well as the visiting athletes.

Hopefully, as time goes on, more governments around the world will invest in disabled athletes, so the responsibility doesn't seem to fall entirely on charities.

I became an athlete thanks to this type of government funding. I was spotted as having potential because of a scheme which was looking for talented disabled athletes. Without this opportunity, I don't think I'd have considered sport as a career option. But none of this had happened to me yet. It wasn't even a hobby at that point!

7. Playground to podium

In 2007, my family moved from London to Bath. This coincided with me leaving Year Six and starting secondary school. I'd have to wear a uniform for the first time ever and it was a girls' school, not mixed like my primary school. It felt daunting turning up not knowing anyone from my previous school, but I needn't have worried. I made some lovely friends in the first term and most of them were arty, not sporty.

PE suddenly became a popularity contest – who would be picked first for each team – that was somehow both stressful *and* boring at the same time. I hated most of the games we played and netball was probably the worst.

I always had to be the goalkeeper because my prosthetic leg was too uncomfortable, and I couldn't run for long periods of time. The problem was, I was one of the shortest in the class and never managed to save a goal. It was the same in football and hockey. Sometimes, the ball would bounce off my fake leg and I'd save a goal by accident, but my actual skill level never improved. I was often picked last, which wasn't fun. I was more likely to be found sitting down making the world's longest daisy chain than properly taking part in rounders.

When I was 12, my PE teacher suggested I attend a sports event just for disabled students. It was called "Playground to Podium" and the aim was to find the next generation of Paralympians by giving us the opportunity to try out lots of different sports. The part that persuaded me the most was the fact I'd get to miss a whole day of school!

I was a bit nervous because I didn't know anyone – I was the only student with a physical disability in my whole school. But missing double maths was such an incredible incentive, I forced myself to go. It would be the first time I'd be participating in sports with other disabled kids. I wouldn't have to feel like the odd one out who no one wanted on their team.

I tried loads of different sports: table tennis, athletics, seated ice hockey, fencing, boccia, wheelchair basketball, trampolining, swimming, sitting volleyball, football – and probably a few I've forgotten. I made friends with a girl called Alice and I started throwing myself into the new sports with a bit more enthusiasm.

I *knew* I wasn't great at most sports; anything involving a ball and a team was a disaster. I wear strong prescription glasses, so my peripheral vision is almost non-existent – anything (human or object) coming at me from the side was a complete shock! But I was good at sprinting in short bursts, zooming around in a wheelchair, climbing and being extremely bendy.

At 14, I went to an athletics taster day. I liked sprinting, even though running in a prosthetic was tough. Alice was there too. Her cerebral palsy affected one side of her body, so we had similar asymmetrical running styles. Cerebral palsy (CP) is a type of brain condition that impacts balance, coordination and strength. We raced the 100 metres, and someone timed us with a stopwatch.

My 100 metre time was recorded at around 16 seconds. I was told that was pretty good for an amputee without a running blade (a special lower limb made from layers of carbon fibre). It felt really exciting: proof that I was actually decent at sprinting. Being the only amputee at my school often made me feel inferior in PE. Deep down,

I knew I was strong and fast, but I rarely got to show it, especially when I was always stuck in goal. On the rare occasions we got to sprint at school, I usually did OK against the others, but I never really got that feeling of *winning*.

Now, there was a real chance that I'd get to race people with the same disability as me. I'd be able to see where I stood in the world rankings and figure out how far off I was from a Paralympic qualifying time. I'd finally have the chance to compete in a fair race.

This was probably the bit I was most looking forward to. It's such a simple thing, but I'd never been in a running race that was equal before. Even in those early days, I think I knew I'd found the right sport for me. No teammates to feel bad about letting down, no flying objects hitting me in the face. Just me, in a lane, on a running track.

A talent-spotter from England Athletics had seen potential in me and Alice. He helped us find a coach at Bath University, someone who already trained Paralympians. That gave me a huge boost of confidence – I was in the right place. If I could get my hands on a proper running blade, maybe the Paralympics weren't just a dream. Not 2012, which was two years away, but maybe Rio 2016.

Alice and I joined a training group at Bath University, and I started going three times a week. My coach, Rob, quickly realised that endurance events, where I had to run long distances, weren't going to work for me, so we focused on sprints and worked around my limitations. I also started applying for funding for a proper running blade. Training was great. Alice and I were the only teenagers in the group, but even though everyone else was university-age or older, we were totally included.

There were only two strict rules at training: we weren't allowed to use the word "can't" and no false starting. If coach Rob heard anyone say this forbidden word or witnessed a false start, the offender was fined. This meant either running 300 metres multiple times or bringing sweets or chocolate to share with everyone at the next training session. Sometimes athletes brought in treats just to be nice, so there was generally some form of sugar to keep you going in a hard session. It was a fun, positive environment.

To compete internationally against athletes with similar impairments, I needed to be officially classified. Classification is where athletes like me are placed in the most appropriate group for competing. A group of trained professionals check medical documents and assess each athlete's impairment. Then they observe how the athlete competes. There was a classification event in Cardiff in June 2011, which wasn't too far from Bath. I didn't have a running blade yet, but that didn't matter, I could still get classified without one.

The process was simple in my case: the assessment of my leg confirmed that, yes, my foot was missing.

Then I was observed in competition (presumably to double-check that it was still missing when I ran). Alice was getting classified too, and we ended up in the same 100 metre race.

After the race, we found out our times and classifications. I was a T44. The "T" stands for Track and 44 refers to athletes with a single below-knee amputation or similar impairments, like a fused ankle. Alice was classified as a T37, a category for athletes with coordination impairments affecting one side of the body.

My time for that race was 17.22 seconds. I can't lie; I felt a bit disappointed. I knew the 16-second time I'd run before wasn't very accurate, but part of me still felt like I'd got slower. It didn't really matter, though. I didn't have a running blade yet, and I had no clue how to use starting blocks. These are adjustable footrests that sit behind the start line and help athletes push off with more stability and speed than a simple standing start. They're also hooked up to a mechanism that detects false starts. I had only been training for a matter of months! There was so much to improve upon. I was excited to see how much faster I could run with a blade.

8. Classifications and competitions

If you've ever watched the Paralympics, you've probably noticed that in some events, like swimming, athletes with very different impairments often compete in the same race. You might see someone with moderate cerebral palsy racing alongside someone with a double leg amputation, and wonder if it's fair.

That's where the classification system comes in. Classification is designed to make competition as fair as possible. Paralympians are grouped based on how their impairments affect their ability to perform in that specific sport. Athletes within the same category should have roughly the same level of function, even if their disabilities are completely different.

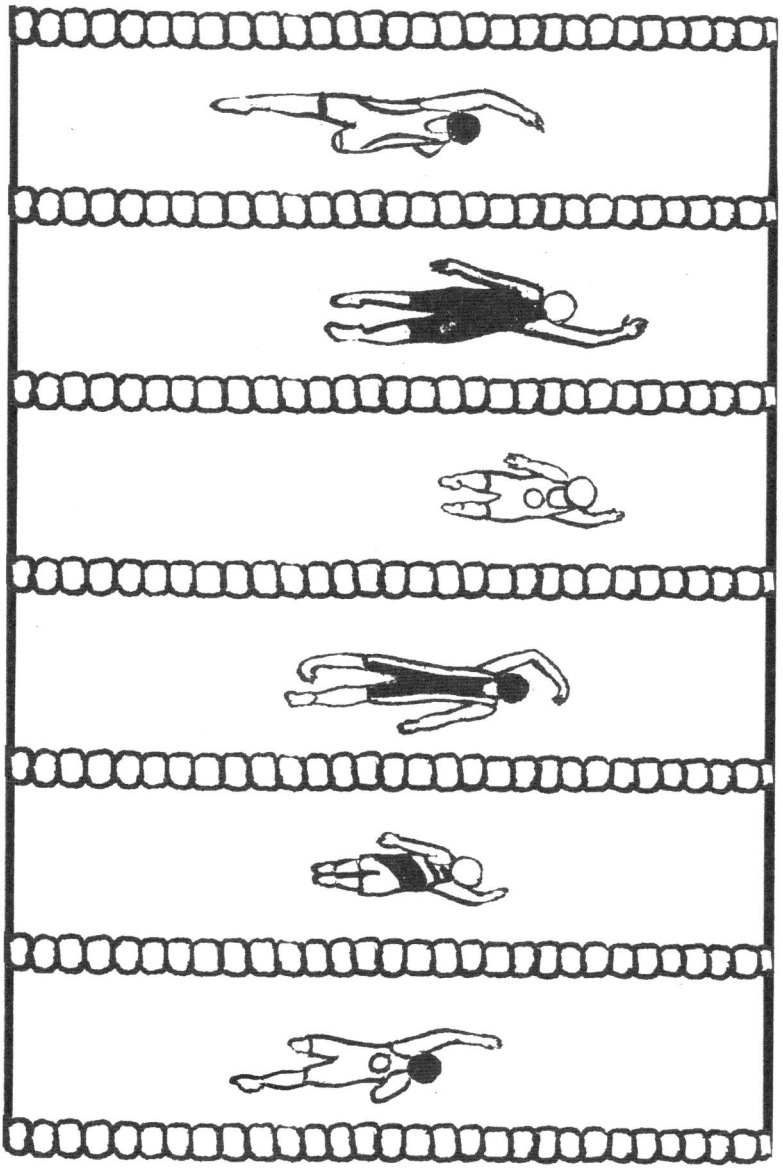

Athletics is a little different and tends to group similar disabilities together; you won't find anyone with one arm competing against someone with one leg.

However, at local level, because there weren't many women in the same category as me in the UK, it wouldn't be unusual for me to find myself in the same race as athletes with visual impairments, cerebral palsy, or arm amputations! Competition organisers do their best to group similar disabilities together, but that often wasn't an option.

Classification is by no means perfect: it's complex and often controversial. While it's based on medical assessments and scientific testing, classifiers don't always get it right. Some disabilities, like amputation or visual impairment, are relatively straightforward to measure. Is the limb missing? Can you see a certain distance? Simple yes or no questions.

But when a disability exists on a spectrum, like cerebral palsy, things get much trickier.

Occasionally, athletes are put into the wrong category, and this might mean that they're at a major advantage OR a major disadvantage.

When an athlete is classified incorrectly, the best-case scenario is that the issue is recognised quickly, they are reclassified and put in the right category to maintain fairness. Unfortunately this doesn't always happen.

In some cases, athletes may have to change classification if their condition worsens. A visually impaired swimmer might begin their career in one category but move to another category if their condition deteriorates.

During the London 2012 Paralympics, each event was introduced with a graphic called LEXI, designed to explain the classifications. It used colour coding to show how much different parts of the body were affected. Every sport has a different system using different letters and numbers, so it would have been impossible for viewers to know what was going on without it.

It's really important that spectators understand how Paralympians with different impairments are grouped together. Then they can appreciate the skill, strategy and effort each athlete, regardless of their impairment, brings to their sport.

9. London 2012, here I come!

In the autumn after my classification, I got a running blade. My mum had helped me apply for funding from a charity called "READY", who help pay for sports equipment for young disabled people. We were hoping they'd help to partially fund my blade, but they said they'd pay for the whole thing! This was such an exciting boost for my confidence; I'd said in my application that I hoped to compete for my country one day, and they believed in me enough to give me thousands of pounds for a running blade!

I went to a private company to have my running prosthetic made. The socket (the bit that the stump goes into) is the most expensive part because it takes a lot of people many hours to make sure it fits properly. The bouncy blade part is still expensive, but I imagine most people don't expect it to be that way round. In total, it ended up costing about £3,600. I will always be so grateful to "READY" for taking that chance on me.

Training using a running blade was so much more fun than my "day" leg. Instead of feeling like I was running with a brick rather than a foot, it was like having a spring! I got used to it very quickly and could do a lot more sprinting because my stump didn't hurt from the impact anymore.

I was so excited to see how my 100 metre time had changed after nearly a year of training and around six months on a blade. The difference was massive. In April 2012, I ran 14.50 seconds, a huge improvement from 17.22 seconds the year before. Annoyingly, the time didn't technically count because there was a tailwind of 2.9. A tailwind means the wind is blowing in the same direction as you are running in. Anything above 2.0 is seen as giving the sprinter an advantage. So, although I was extremely pleased with my progress, the time wouldn't count towards qualification.

My next competition was in May 2012. It was a big one. I had been selected to compete for Great Britain in an event in Manchester called the Paralympic World Cup, in the 100 metre and 200 metre races. Athletes from all over the world would be there, including other T44s, to race against. At last, a fair race! I was starting to think maybe the London 2012 Paralympics might not be so unrealistic. If I could do well here, maybe I could get a place on the British team.

I met some of the athletes I'd be competing against, and in a way that was more daunting than the actual races. So far, I hadn't really felt nervous about competing, but meeting all these proper grown-up Paralympic athletes and record holders was intimidating!

The 100 metre race went OK and I got a new personal best time of 14.10 seconds. There was a tailwind, but it was only 0.6, so the time counted. For pretty much the whole race, I was in third position, but right at the last second, another athlete ran past me to get the bronze! I was so annoyed with myself – if only I'd dipped at the line! Dipping is a surprisingly tricky move that sprinters use right before the finish line in a really close race. They bend forward at the waist so their torso crosses the line first – that's what decides the winner! But if they mistime it, they could lose their balance and fall, so it's a bit risky. I didn't really know how to do that yet, but still! I had to tell myself that fourth in my first international race is still pretty good, and nothing to be ashamed of.

Next up was the 200 metre race, and a chance to aim higher. The only problem was that I absolutely hated this distance. It's way too far and my legs and lungs always got so incredibly tired in the second half. As I predicted, I didn't enjoy the experience of the second half of the race, but I remembered the instructions from my coach to focus on staying relaxed and keeping my hands and knees up.

I was exhausted as I crossed the line, but that didn't bother me as much as it usually did because I got the bronze medal! An international medal in my second ever 200 metre race! *And* we were running into a -2.0 headwind (that's when the wind is blowing towards you, which makes running even more tiring!). I was still slightly annoyed about the 100 metres, but I knew I could improve.

In June, I competed in the 100 metre race again – this time in Watford – and I was back to racing non-disabled athletes. Some competitions use something called "seeding". This means competitors are judged by how fast they can run a particular distance. If a 12-year-old boy and a 60-year-old woman have similar 100 metre times, they can race against each other – age, gender or disability are not taken into account using this system. I surprised myself by coming second. I got a new personal best of 13.90 seconds, and became the new British record holder. I was definitely getting selected for the London 2012 Paralympics now!

10. Spotlight on London

The London 2012 Paralympics was a game changer. About 2.7 million tickets were sold. The media interest was extensive, with more live coverage than ever before. Over 100 countries broadcast the Games, reaching around four billion viewers worldwide. It wasn't just the numbers that were different, it was the whole atmosphere. The general public's enthusiasm filled stadiums *and* changed the way people thought about disability and sport.

One of the things I enjoyed most about the Paralympics (aside from being in it) was *The Last Leg*, a nightly comedy TV show that discussed and celebrated that day's sporting events. Two out of the three hosts were disabled. That kind of representation on a comedy show had rarely been seen before, and it was popular, averaging 1.2 million viewers a night.

Many British Paralympians were inspired by what they saw in the media during London 2012. Seeing yourself represented can be so uplifting and inspiring for *all* disabled children (and adults), who might have otherwise thought sport wasn't for them.

I remember really wanting to watch more of *The Last Leg*, but as it started at 10 p.m., I was often getting ready for bed (sleep is very important for athletes).

Channel 4 also put up posters with the slogan: "Thanks for the warm-up", referring to the Olympics and implying the Paralympics was the main event. I absolutely loved this; the Paralympics had so often been seen as a bit of an afterthought, a wholesome event for disabled people to give it a go … Not this time. Paralympians were finally being framed as elite athletes.

As well as the TV coverage, some athletes used social media to promote the Paralympics.

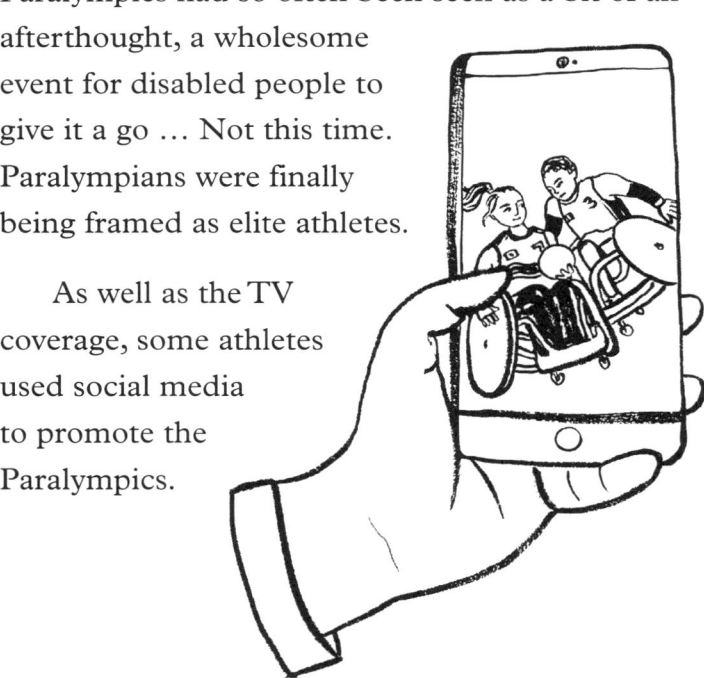

It was a chance for each athlete to choose how to present themselves and their sport, from funny stories to more serious discussions about mental health. Having lots of followers on social media means Paralympians have a better chance of gaining sponsorship from businesses, too.

I feel so privileged to have been able to take part in the Paralympic Games that finally gave disabled athletes the coverage and crowds they deserved. So many things had to fall into place for me to get there: being born with tibia hemimelia, becoming an elective amputee, the Playground to Podium events, being noticed by England Athletics, a brilliant coach, supportive parents and receiving a charity-funded running blade. So much of it came down to luck, and being in the right place at the right time.

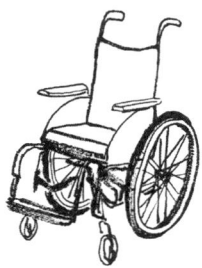

11. My Paralympics London 2012

I only let myself believe I was really going to the Paralympics when I got the official phone call to tell me I'd been selected. I'd been chosen to compete in the 100 metre race (*yay!*) and the 200 metre race (*yuck*). Then it was just a whirlwind, going to London for the launch party, getting fitted for the GB kit, and being in a huge group photo with the whole team.

Before the Games began, we flew to Portugal for warm-weather training. Training somewhere warm is great for athletes. The higher temperature helps to loosen muscles, and that means we can run a bit faster! New athletes (like me) also got a chance to get to know everyone on the team. It was a *lot* warmer than the conditions I was used to, and I suffered from heat exhaustion. I celebrated my sixteenth birthday while I was in Portugal, but I felt too unwell to eat. I only managed a few grains of plain rice and some cucumber for dinner. I couldn't even touch my birthday cake.

Three days later, my mum phoned. She had just gone into school to collect my GCSE results, and as she went through them one by one, I was pleasantly surprised. An A★ in History. There must be some mistake! An A in Chemistry? You've got to be joking me! Bs in Maths and Physics. I was convinced I'd be lucky to get Cs in those! I had revised diligently, but I'd also been training six times a week throughout study leave. There was a part of me that knew I probably could have done a bit more if I'd had the energy to stay up later. These results meant that my hard work had paid off. Hopefully, the effort I'd put into training would pay off too and I'd make it into at least one final!

When the training camp was over, we flew back to London and went straight into the Olympic/Paralympic Village. This is the best place in the world – it's a shame that it only exists for about three weeks every four years. It's the only time in my life where being disabled didn't put me in the minority. In the Paralympic Village, the disabled people outnumbered the non-disabled people, and it was incredible! Every type of mobility aid was represented, every area was fully accessible and, best of all, no one demanded to know what happened to my leg. Instead, people asked what event I was competing in or offered to swap pin badges. Every country's team has a unique pin badge and exchanging them is a nice way to start a conversation.

I was the youngest on the team and I felt lucky there wasn't a lot of pressure on me. While other athletes had to manage the expectation of winning medals, I did not. My coach's only goal for me was to reach both finals, that was all I needed to focus on.

The thing about sprinting is, you have to focus on yourself and your own race. You can't get distracted by the other athletes, or the rubbish weather. You can't control any of that and stressing about things you have no control over is pointless and will probably make you run slower.

When a large number of athletes are competing at the same distance (like the 100 metres), they're divided into smaller groups, called heats. There were two heats for my race – the first three athletes to cross the finishing line in each heat automatically got a place in the final race. The last two spaces in the final were for the "fastest losers". This could be one athlete from each heat, or two from one heat, depending on how fast their time is.

The call room is where athletes are held before stepping out on the track. You have to be in there for quite a while with everyone you're about to compete against. It was quite strange, sitting on plastic chairs under all the stadium seating, hearing the muffled roar of the crowds and watching your competitors jump up and down to try to stay warm. I brought a book to read because call room rules mean if you're caught with anything electronic, like a mobile phone or a smart watch, you get disqualified. I think we'd have all loved to be listening to music, but that wasn't an option. My book caused a bit of a stir because my competitors couldn't believe I was calm enough to read!

Getting onto the track for the first time in my 100 metre heat was mind-blowing. The stadium was full to the brim, the crowd was loud and there seemed to be a load of flashing lights everywhere. I had to do my best to ignore the fact that I'd be running in front of 80,000 people and calmly set up my starting blocks. You get one practice go with your blocks to make sure you've set them up properly. After that, you have to stand behind them and patiently wait for a camera to be aimed at your face as you get introduced to the crowd.

I was in lane five. Often, in the heats, they don't show each starting athlete individually, but I knew they'd definitely show me because I was British, and wow, did the crowd give me their support! They had no idea who I was, but they were supporting me because of the flag I was wearing on my kit. I felt a bit silly. I could see myself on one of the big screens and was hardly able to stop smiling; it was unlike anything I'd ever experienced.

My coach told me that once I'd finished waving at the camera, I needed to focus on my next move – getting into the blocks and then getting out of them really fast (*after* the starting gun, of course). So, that's what I did – after waving and smiling to the camera, I looked straight ahead, until they called:

"On your marks." That's when you get into your starting position.

"Get set." That's when you raise your bottom in the air.

BANG! Once you hear the starting gun you run as fast as you possibly can.

I came fourth in my heat with a time of 14.11 seconds. If my time was fast enough, I would get one of the two extra places in the final, but I wouldn't know if I'd made it until the second heat had finished. There was a chance that this would be the end of my 100 metre Paralympic journey. It was an agonising wait. I really wanted to run the 100 metres again. It was so much fun having such incredible support and racing against athletes from all over the world.

When the results of the second heat finally went up, I felt a flood of relief. My fourth place time was good enough! I'd completed my mission of making a Paralympic final. My main aim now was to not come last.

I was on the inside lane for the final – the lane draws for the final take into account the speeds in the heat. As I had been the slowest qualifier, I was on the edge, with the fastest athletes in the middle lanes. Being right on the edge is considered a bit of a disadvantage because you aren't surrounded by competitors. I had one athlete on my right and an empty space to my left.

The camera zoomed in on me first and yet again, the home crowd delivered. I did the expected waving and smiling, still finding it strange that my face was on a massive screen in the stadium, as well as on televisions all over the world. Then I had to get my head back in the game.

I don't actually remember anything about this race. If you're sprinting well, it's very difficult to recall any specific details. Some people call this an out-of-body experience. Despite the roaring crowd, I didn't hear a thing while I was sprinting. I ended up coming fifth with a time of 13.98 seconds. I was happy to have raced under 14 seconds, and to go from the slowest runner to qualify, to fifth place.

I got to do it all over again in the 200 metre race. This time I wore a big white flower hair clip which the commentators noticed, and they suggested it might impact my running. The reason I'm slow in the 200 metres has nothing to do with my hairstyle and more to do with the fact it's a tiring race. I finished third in my heat, giving me an automatic place in the final. It was so nice not having to nervously wait for the next heat to see if I'd made it.

The race itself went just as I expected: utterly exhausting. I came sixth. I was pleased with that – I hadn't come last in my least favourite event!

My first Paralympics had been a success. I'd got into both my finals, made friends, and had the best couple of weeks of my life. Being around thousands of Paralympians every day was an incredible part of the experience.

12. Keep on sprinting!

The London 2012 Paralympic Games got me hooked. I wanted to keep competing and see how well I could do. Three A Levels, one Art Foundation course, and a gap year later, it was time to go to the 2016 Olympic Games in Rio de Janeiro, Brazil! I was only racing in the 100 metres this time. I'd had to stop running the 200 metres because it was causing my left foot too much pain – even though I'd managed to get a bronze medal in that event at the 2013 World Championships in Lyon, France.

When the full Paralympic timetable was released I saw that the heat and final were on the same day, and my heart sank. The last time this had happened at an important event had been the year before at the 2015 World Championships in Doha, Qatar. My foot had not liked it! After the final, 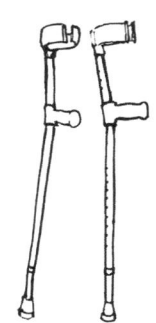 I had found I couldn't bear weight on it due to severe shooting pain. I had ended up needing to use crutches and having to wear a medical boot for eight weeks due to bone stress. Now, my coach changed my training, so there was less impact going through my foot. I no longer had to train to run the 200 metres (no complaints there), but I did have many more bike sessions. With my new training in place, my foot *should* have been able to manage running 100 metres twice in one day.

The heat went well. I not only won the heat, I ran it in a new world record time of 12.93 seconds, beating the world record by 0.05 seconds. I couldn't believe it. I'd run under 13 seconds for the first time in my life, and it was at a Paralympic Games!

The stadium wasn't as packed as London, but my parents and sister were somewhere in the crowd, and the spectators were very noisy and supportive!

I went back to the Paralympic Village to have a lie-down and eat before the evening final. It was going to be my usual bedtime when I'd have to compete, so rest was very important for me. I made one mistake – I watched some TV and one of the commentators said, "… and Sophie Kamlish ran a World Record in the T44 100 metre heats this morning, so that's another guaranteed gold medal in the final!" Had they never watched athletics at the Paralympics before? Nothing is *ever* guaranteed.

Race time came around pretty quickly. With my warm up complete and the long wait in the call room over, I was ready to go. Here's what went through my head after the starting gun went off …

My start was pretty good.

Too good.

Why am I ahead of everyone?

That never happens!

Was there a false start?

No, they'd have fired the gun again by now if there had been.

I'm still in the lead.

I could win.

Oh wait.

I can feel them closing in.

One person's ahead of me.

And another.

And another.

I'm fourth.

Oh no.

As you can see, I had quite a lot going on in my head. The aim for a sprinter is to have nothing on their minds while they're up and running.

This is why I didn't do as well as I should have. I missed out on a medal because overthinking caused my running technique to suffer.

So, I was a world record holder with no medal. It was the best and worst day of my life all rolled into one and I told myself it wouldn't happen again. My coach and I chatted everything through. I needed to get better at ignoring the other athletes around me. I'd tightened up as soon as I heard them running behind me in the final, resulting in my relaxed running style being compromised. In sprinting, relaxed running means fast running.

For every race in the next season, that was what I focused on: ignoring everyone else. The World Para Athletics Championships were in the summer of 2017 and they were held in London. This was very exciting because it was another chance to perform in front of a home crowd. It also meant a lot more pressure. I was going into this major international competition as a world record holder, a favourite to win, and not the usual underdog status I was used to.

The timetable was released, and yet again, my heat and final were on the same day. I wasn't super happy about this – it reminded me too much of my failure in Rio. The heat went well, and I broke my world record with a time of 12.90 seconds. I was delighted but I also felt apprehensive. It was all so similar to 2016, and I really didn't want a repeat of the previous year.

In the break between the heat and the final, I rested like last time, but I avoided all forms of social media, opting for audiobooks, podcasts and music to entertain me instead.

The final started badly, but not for me. Another athlete was disqualified for a false start. False starts, although worse for the offending athlete, aren't good for the other competitors either. Everyone uses up a lot of energy getting out of the blocks and running the first few metres as fast as possible, only to have to walk back and do it all over again. I was lucky in a way; my start hadn't been that good, so I just kept telling myself, *It's fine, you get another chance for a better start.*

My positive self-talk worked; my start was way better the second time round. So was the middle of the race, where I was able to completely block out the feeling of competitors around me. The end was the best part. I crossed the line first, with a pretty big margin between me and second place. An overwhelming feeling of relief washed over me. I was the World Champion. In London! In the very same stadium I'd competed in five years ago at my first Paralympic Games.

13. From sport to art

As soon as I finished competing at the 2016 Paralympics in Rio de Janeiro, I started university. I turned up halfway through the first week, the day after I landed back in England. Lots of athletes choose not to go to university because of how much it disrupts training. I knew it was suddenly going to become a lot more difficult; moving to a different city meant my coach wouldn't be there in person to oversee my sessions and I'd no longer have access to an indoor running track in winter. I'd have to juggle a lot of work *and* try to have a bit of a social life too, while avoiding anything that made me too tired to train properly.

Despite all the difficulties I knew were in store, I still *really* wanted to study Illustration and Animation at Kingston School of Art. Drawing had been my favourite thing to do long before I discovered sprinting, and I knew it would be the career path I'd be going down no matter what. Being an elite professional athlete isn't something you can do for very long. I felt it was important to stay connected with the creative side of my life, so that when I retired from sport, I wouldn't feel lost or scared about an unknown future.

I had a great time at Kingston. I was very busy with work and training. I probably didn't have the most typical university experience because I couldn't really stay out too late or go to parties. To be honest, that wasn't really my thing anyway! I made some great friends who never made me feel guilty about having to rush off to train. Being at university and having so much freedom to choose what to explore with my projects solidified my ambitions to increase disability representation in the media.

After graduating in 2019, I was offered the chance to create an animation for Channel 4; a short piece featuring all the different Paralympic sports. It was supposed to be for social media but it was shown on TV while I was competing in the postponed 2021 Paralympics in Tokyo. I was glad about this because I didn't do very well in the 100 metre final. I came eighth, but at least my animation got to be on TV!

I'm not competing anymore, but I still enjoy sport. It's great to be part of a sporting community, and have more time to spend on creative projects. Not only have I been working as an illustrator and animator, I've also started making and decorating ceramic plates. Art has always been waiting for me to come back and give it my full attention.

We have no idea what the future holds, but I've learnt that saying yes to new things and working hard never goes to waste. Whatever you want to do – give it your best shot!

Book talk questions

What challenges do you think Paralympic athletes face, and how do they overcome them?

How can we prevent ableism against disabled people?

What can be done to improve visibility of the Paralympic Games?

Which sports would you like to see included in the Paralympics?

Are there any Paralympic athletes that you particularly admire?

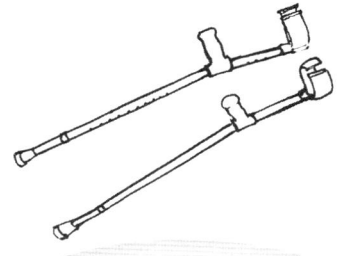

What are your favourite Paralympic sports?

What are classifications in Paralympic Games and how do they work?

What do you think are the qualities of a good athlete?

What new things did you learn while reading this book?

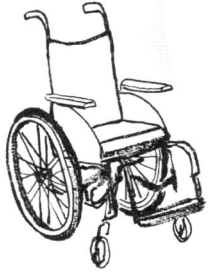

Have you ever seen Sophie competing? What did you think of her performance?

Ask the author

Which moment of your career has impacted you the most?

Competing at London 2012. It showed me a world of possibilities, made me proud to be disabled and encouraged me to work hard for the next four years.

Sophie Kamlish

What did a typical training week look like for you?

I'd train six days a week and no training session was ever the same. I'd have sprint sessions three times a week and bike sessions twice a week. Saturdays were spent in the gym lifting heavy weights – I thought I wouldn't enjoy this, but I loved it!

How did you prepare mentally and physically for competitions?

I'd listen to motivating, upbeat music to help get me in the zone. I always made sure I did a proper hour-long warm-up before a competition, as well as eating enough food and snacks to fuel me for the day.

What motivates you to keep pushing your limits in sports?
I want to be the best athlete I can be, and hopefully inspire a few people out there who don't think sport is for them to give it a try.

Which athlete inspires you the most?
Tatyana McFadden. She got the law changed in her country to make sure disabled children have equal access to high school sports.

What do you think is the most important message from this book?
That the Paralympics deserves more attention and that being disabled is not a bad thing.

What advice would you give to young athletes?
Stick at the sport you enjoy, and if it stops being fun don't force yourself to carry on with it. There are so many sports out there to try!

What are your plans for the future?
I don't compete as a sprinter anymore but I'm hoping to improve at a new sport – climbing! I'll also carry on illustrating and animating, focusing on increasing disability representation.

Published by Collins
An imprint of HarperCollins*Publishers*

The News Building
1 London Bridge Street
London SE1 9GF
UK

Macken House
39/40 Mayor Street Upper
Dublin 1
D01 C9W8
Ireland

Text and illustrations © Sophie Kamlish 2026
Design © HarperCollins*Publishers* Limited 2026

10 9 8 7 6 5 4 3 2 1

ISBN 978-0-00-878473-7

All rights reserved. No part of this publication may be reproduced, stored in a retrieval system, or transmitted in any form by any means, electronic, mechanical, photocopying, recording or otherwise, without the prior written permission of the Publisher or a licence permitting restricted copying in the United Kingdom issued by the Copyright Licensing Agency Ltd, 5th Floor, Shackleton House, 4 Battle Bridge Lane, London SE1 2HX.

Without limiting the exclusive rights of any author, contributor or the publisher of this publication, any unauthorised use of this publication to train generative artificial intelligence (AI) technologies is expressly prohibited. HarperCollins also exercise their rights under Article 4(3) of the Digital Single Market Directive 2019/790 and expressly reserve this publication from the text and data mining exception.

British Library Cataloguing-in-Publication Data
A catalogue record for this publication is available from the British Library.

Author and illustrator: Sophie Kamlish
Publisher: Laura White
Commissioning editor: Holly Woolnough
Development editor: Zoë Clarke
Product manager: Holly Woolnough
Content editor: Selin Akca
Copyeditor: Catherine Dakin

Proofreaders: Sally Byford, Sasha Morton
Reviewer: Lisa Davis
Fact checker: Sasha Morton
Cover designer: Sarah Finan
Internal designer: 2Hoots Publishing Services Ltd
Typesetter: David Jimenez
Production controller: Sophie Waeland

Collins would like to thank the teachers and children at Grange Primary School, Southwark, for being part of the development of Big Cat Read On.

Printed in the UK

Made with responsibly sourced paper and vegetable ink

Scan to see how we are reducing our environmental impact.

Get the latest Collins Big Cat news at
collins.co.uk/collinsbigcat

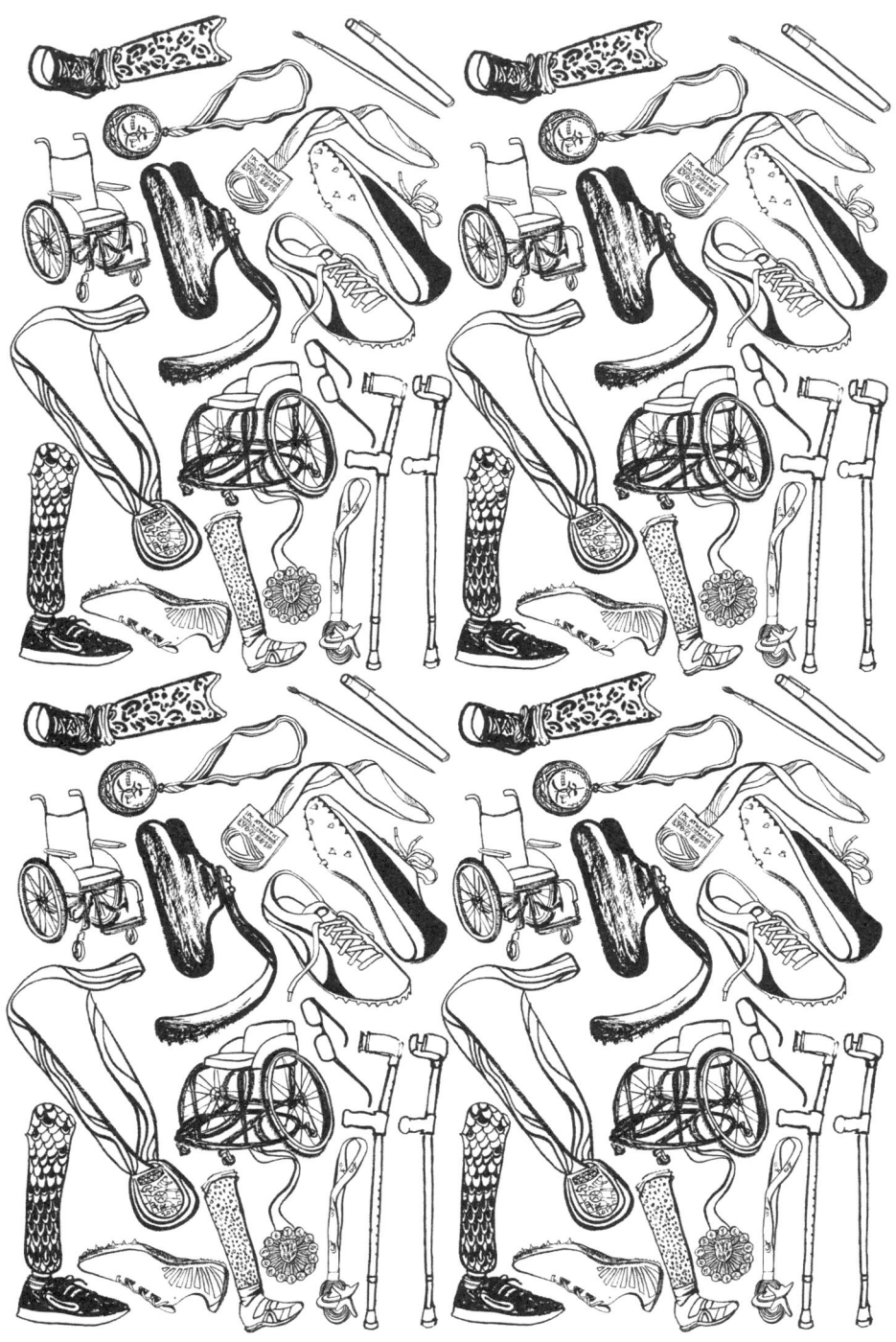

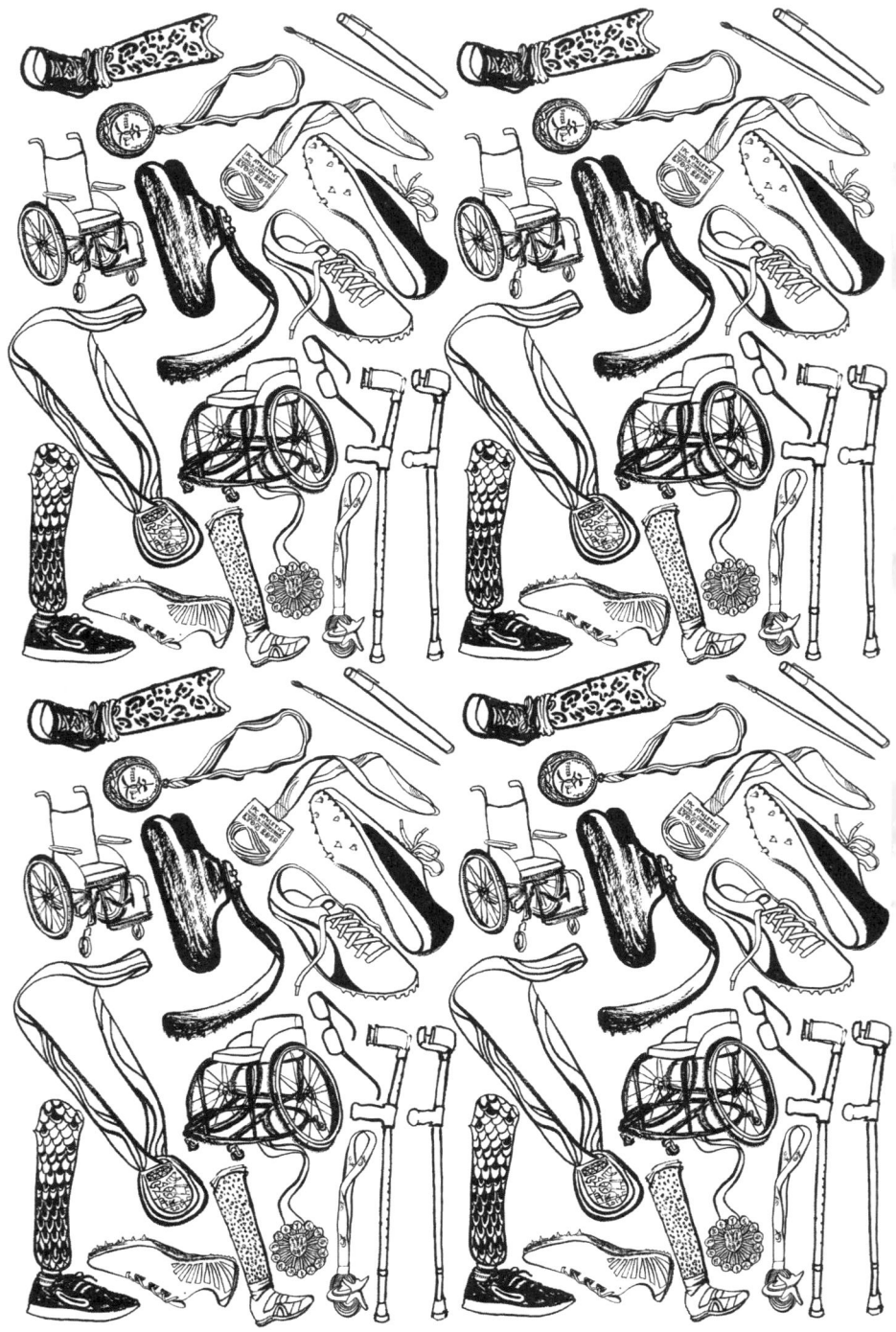